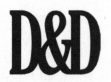

ELEVATE YOUR WINE EXPERIENCE WITH OUR JOURNALS AND LOGBOOKS

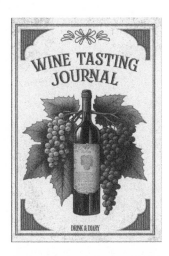

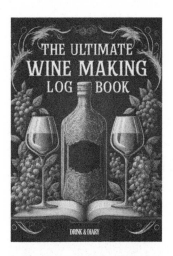

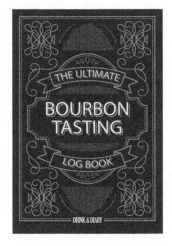

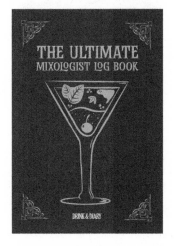

Visit Our Amazon Store

amazon.com/author/drinkanddiary

This Journal Belongs To

_____

Made in United States
Orlando, FL
02 February 2023

29388532R00082